Original title:

Heaven at the Shore

Copyright © 2025 Creative Arts Management OÜ
All rights reserved.

Author: Matthew Whitaker
ISBN HARDBACK: 978-1-80581-642-3
ISBN PAPERBACK: 978-1-80581-169-5
ISBN EBOOK: 978-1-80581-642-3

Whispers of Celestial Waves

The seagulls squawk with flair,
While beach balls soar through air.
Sandcastles made with laughter,
Waves bring joy, ever after.

Flip-flops dance with each small wave,
In this sandy, sunny grave.
Turtles in their shells so grand,
Join the party on our land.

Beneath the Infinite Sky

Clouds are shaped like giant pies,
Kites take flight with funny sighs.
Sunburnt noses, silly hats,
Dance like goofy acrobats.

Chasing waves with all our might,
Splashing friends is pure delight.
The sunbeam tickles on our toes,
While friendship in the breeze flows.

The Tranquil Embrace of Tides

A crab that scuttles, oh so quick,
Winks at the fish; what a trick!
Jellyfish glide with grace untold,
In this ocean of laughs, behold.

Seashells whisper, tales of woe,
While ice cream drips, we're still aglow.
Pelicans dive with comic glee,
Sharing snacks for all to see.

Celestial Horizons and Sandy Dreams

Mermaids gossip, that's the scoop,
While dolphins join our ocean troop.
With wave-washed feet and salty cheer,
We'll dance till nightfall, never fear.

Starfish laugh upon the sand,
As we try to build the tallest stand.
The moon invites us to the show,
As starlit wishes start to glow.

Dreams Linger on Ocean Breezes

A crab in a suit, prancing with flair,
He thinks he's the star, with nary a care.
Seagulls form bands, singing off-key,
While fish start to dance, and giggle with glee.

The sandcastles sway, they topple with grace,
Turtles wearing shades are winning the race.
With jellyfish hip-hop, the tide starts to rise,
And laughter erupts under sunny blue skies.

Waves of Serenity and Celestial Light

The sea laughs aloud, as waves tickle toes,
Shells gossip the secrets that nobody knows.
Octopuses juggle, and dolphins take bets,
As seagulls do yoga, and stretch without pets.

A fisherman's wish, he catches a shoe,
And wonders if fish have a shoe store or two.
The sunrise paints smiles on each sunny face,
While starfish hold meetings about outer space.

Mystical Shores under Moonlit Skies

Mermaids are giggling, tossing their hair,
As pirates play tag; oh, what a weird pair!
The tides come in softly, like a warm hug,
While crabs give high-fives, all snug in the rug.

The moon winks at sandcastles, crafty and bold,
While shells trade tall tales of treasures untold.
The breeze offers jokes, wrapped in salty delight,
As surfboards share secrets on this starry night.

The Ethereal Dance of Wind and Water

Kites dance and twirl, caught in the breeze,
As children compete for the best peanut seas.
The breeze tells the waves, 'Please do a twirl!',
While buckets of joy cause each moment to swirl.

The clouds wear sunglasses, they chill just right,
While seashells pass gossip about the moon's height.
Waves pull the laughter, they bounce, they collide,
As everyone grins, swept up in the ride.

Serenity's Embrace

On the beach, I found a crab,
He danced like he was in a fab.
With tiny feet and funny flair,
He waved to clouds without a care.

Seagulls squawk, a comedy show,
Trying to steal my sandwich, oh no!
They plot with stealth, wings in a flap,
While I just watch, laughing, and clap.

Whispers of the Celestial Sea

A fish jumped high, missed its cue,
Landed right in my shoes, how rude!
With bubbles popping, it made its plea,
'Help me out, I'm not meant to be!'

The waves rolled in, like a slapstick act,
Splashing my towel, and that's a fact!
I dodged the foam, in a silly dance,
While the tide chuckled at my mischance.

Twilight's Coastal Dream

The sun set low, a golden glow,
I tripped on sand, oh no, oh no!
Rolling like a tumbleweed, I fell,
A seagull laughed, 'Do tell, do tell!'

Beach balls flew in a wacky game,
One hit me hard, a rounder name!
I bounced right back, with humor bright,
'A beach bum shows up, a funny sight!'

Paradise Found in Sand

A sandcastle rose, with towers so grand,
But it melted fast, just like my plans.
The tide came in, a sneaky thief,
Saying, 'Bye-bye, here's your reef!'

My friend built one that looked like a bear,
But the waves came to declare, 'That's unfair!'
We laughed as it splashed, a fuzzy attack,
Leaving our joy to make a comeback.

Coastal Reveries

Seagulls squawk like they own the place,
As beach balls bounce and race.
A kid slips on a sandy hill,
While trying to catch a fragrant thrill.

Crabs march like a tiny army,
In search of dreams quite balmy.
Umbrellas tilt in the sea breeze,
While sunscreen battles the waves with ease.

A dolphin jumps, did you see that?
Was it a show or just a prat?
Flip-flops flop like fish outta water,
The laughter echoes, oh, how it's slaughtered!

So here we sit, and giggle some,
As waves crash loud, and we all hum.
The sunset paints us like a brush,
In this madcap seaside rush.

Celestial Caresses

Stars peek out like eyes so sly,
While jellyfish dance, oh my, oh my!
A beach chair tilts, what a sight,
As someone spills their soda light.

Sandcastles rise, then tumble down,
Like goofy kings with paper crowns.
The tide pulls back, then gives a shove,
A game we play with nudging love.

Flip-flop furies and sandy feet,
Gathering shells that smell quite sweet.
We chase our dreams along the shore,
But maybe we'll find snacks galore!

Gazing up with slightly squinted eyes,
We laugh at friends, and their silly lies.
The night gets louder with each flicker,
And we re-rise after the snicker.

The Divine Melody of Ocean Whispers

Waves hum tunes like old, wise souls,
As we dig for treasure in sandy bowls.
A kite twirls above in a dizzy spin,
While some try to tan, and many chagrin.

Seashells clink like coins from a chest,
While beachgoers put their patience to test.
A hermit crab's on a stroll so slow,
While a child giggles and runs to throw.

The ice cream melts in the summer heat,
And that dog steals a burger—what a feat!
We wave at boats like they're our pals,
Trying to catch the breeze that always Scowls.

As sun drops low, laughter swells,
With stories shared like ocean swells.
We dance with joy on this sandy floor,
And giggle loud, we all want more.

Reflections of Light on Rippling Waters

Morning's light glimmers like winks from fate,
While beachgoers gather and contemplate.
The waves splash around like puppies at play,
Tugging at troubles, whisking them away.

A fish jumps high, and so do we,
Squeals of laughter are wild and free.
Sand everywhere, it's losing the fight,
But hey, that's the joy of this sunny plight.

A picnic blanket flaps like a flag,
While chips go flying, oh what a snag!
Seagulls dive-bomb just like our dreams,
Stealing our snacks, or so it seems.

As twilight's glow makes the sky sigh,
We toast to the stars, already nearby.
In this silly tale of laughter galore,
We'll spin stories 'til we can't anymore.

Where the Sea Kisses the Stars

The ocean wore a goofy grin,
As waves danced with a fish's fin.
The stars fell down like silly confetti,
While crabs played tag, all bright and petty.

A seagull squawked its latest joke,
While jellyfish did a wobbly poke.
The moon chuckled, hanging high,
As starfish told tales with a dreamy sigh.

Elysian Dunes and Twilight Glows

In the twilight, shadows twirled,
As sandcastles proudly unfurled.
Dune bunnies wore sun hats with flair,
Dreaming of carrots and salty air.

The breeze tickled toes with a laugh,
As children played their silly craft.
Seashells giggled beneath the sun,
Holding secrets of beachy fun.

The Otherworldly Symphony of Surf

The surf sang a tune full of glee,
While dolphins danced with cups of tea.
Crabby conductors waved their claws,
Leading the beach-side round of applause.

A starfish played a ukulele bright,
Under the glow of the soft moonlight.
Waves clapped hands, a rhythmic cheer,
As laughter bubbled up from here.

Starlit Sands and Seraphic Breezes

Amidst starlit grains that sparkled so,
Sand monsters strutted, putting on a show.
The breeze wore sunglasses, oh what a sight,
Whispering jokes to the moon at night.

An octopus juggled shells with grace,
While sea turtles joined in a slow race.
With laughter echoing through the light,
The beach became our playful night.

A Mirrored Horizon of Dreams and Stars

The seagulls wear their shades, it's true,
Taking selfies with the ocean blue.
Crabs are snapping photos, you'll see,
While jellyfish dance in glee at the spree.

Shells whisper secrets to the grains of sand,
Waves tumble gently, that's the plan.
Flip-flops flying, watch them soar,
As beach balls bounce and laughter roars.

The Luminous Path of the Wandering Tide.

Starfish strut with swagger and flair,
As surfboards line up without a care.
An octopus plays the ukulele tight,
While dolphins throw a poolside night.

Mermaids sip smoothies on the rocks,
With flip-flop parties, no time for clocks.
The tide rolls in, a grand parade,
Every wave a punchline, perfectly laid.

Elysium by the Waves

Seagulls jest with a witty squawk,
While beach umbrellas bloom like a walk.
Sandcastles built with bucket and pail,
Stand proudly tall, telling tales without fail.

The sun wears sunglasses, what a sight!
And crabs practice tap dance with delight.
With squirrels stealing chips from the spread,
Every moment's comedy, just ahead!

Celestial Tides

The waves hum a tune, a playful tease,
As kids frolic in foamy seas.
Starfish wiggle and try to swim,
While the sunset gives the day a whim.

Beach towels spread like laughter's embrace,
Sunburns and giggles race in the space.
With jellybeans hidden under a shell,
Every tide's a joke better than well.

Glimmers of Divine Serenity

The sun slips into the sea,
A fish wearing sunglasses, you see.
He winks with a smile so wide,
While seagulls laugh, they take a ride.

Flip-flops dance upon the sand,
A crab starts its conga band.
With each wave, a joke does flow,
The jellyfish laughs, 'Ain't this a show?'

The sky wraps us in a blue embrace,
While starfish play tag, just in case.
A snail in a shell takes a break,
Shouting, 'I'm just here for the cake!'

So grab your float and take a dip,
Enjoy the giggles, let laughter rip.
For laughter at this shore is a thrill,
With cosmic humor, we all fulfill.

The Realm of Distant Dreams

Clouds form shapes of goofy smiles,
A dolphin's dance just travels miles.
While seashells sing their silly tunes,
And crabs wear hats made from spoons.

A kite flies high, pulled by the wind,
It flops and flails, what a funny trend!
With flip-flops stuck in the sand,
A hermit crab commands the band.

A starfish prances, quite the sight,
Wiggling its arms, a true delight.
The waves whisper secrets to the foam,
Inviting all to feel at home.

So laugh with the tide, let joy awake,
In this land of dreams, we take a break.
With quirky antics all around,
In this realm, pure joy is found!

Echoes of Celestial Whispers

The moon giggles, a glowing tease,
Caught in waves like a dance with ease.
A crab recites poetry with flair,
While sea turtles join in the air.

Stars fall like confetti at night,
As dolphins do backflips, what a sight!
A seaweed wiggle makes everyone grin,
While a clam yells, "Hey, let the fun begin!"

Clouds tickle the sun, a game of chase,
With jellybean raindrops at a rapid pace.
Where fish wear crowns, oh what a ball,
In the pool of laughter, we share it all.

So gather around this shimmering pool,
With chuckles and jests, let's all be cool.
For echoes of joy, let's spread them wide,
In this cosmic caper, let's take a ride!

Shores of Ethereal Wonder

Mermaids drop their makeup bags,
As giggles burst from playful jags.
The sand is soft, a feather bed,
Where all the laughter is brightly spread.

A turtle tells a tall-tale or two,
About adventures that people never knew.
With seashell trumpets blaring out tunes,
While sandcastles dance beneath the moons.

A pelican's grace is quite supreme,
Flipping fish like it's a dream.
The tide rolls in with a silly cheer,
Whispering secrets for all to hear.

So join this wild, whimsical spree,
On shores of giggles, come ride with me.
With every wave, a chuckle swells,
In this realm of joy, every heart dwells!

Sunlit Promises by the Bay

Seagulls squawk like they own the place,
Kids building castles, all anchored with grace.
The ice cream melts down a sandy cone,
While crabs dig holes to claim as their throne.

Flip-flops flapping, a dance on the run,
Sunscreen battles with rays and just one.
A beach ball flies like a UFO's map,
As laughter erupts from a sunburned chap.

Sandcastles crumble with waves on a march,
Enticing the sea with a wobbly arch.
Tanned people squint at the radar of fun,
"Look, a dolphin!"—but it's just a bun.

In this playground where joy is the plan,
Seashells keep secrets until they can't.
Bubbles emerge, floating high like a kite,
While toddlers chase dreams in the warm sunlight.

The Horizon's Lullaby

The breeze whispers tales of lost pirate gold,
While fishermen toss lines, full of stories untold.
Sandwiches squished in a cooler so wide,
A pelican swoops, stealing lunch with great pride.

Tanning too hard, my stripes might just stick,
Imitating dolphins with one funny trick.
A sunburned buddy, his dance is a sight,
Twisting and turning, he's lost in the light.

Building our dreams with each wave that breaks,
"Is that a whale?" "Nah, it's Fred's goofy shakes!"
The lighthouse stands tall, keeping watch and a grin,
As beach goers wander, let the fun begin.

With laughter as salty as the water we splash,
Each moment's a treasure, now hurry, make haste.
The horizon keeps chuckling, a bright amulet,
As we dance with the sunset—no worries, no debt.

Mystical Tides at Dusk

Evening falls quiet with a splash and a sigh,
The waves hold secrets beneath a pink sky.
Starfish perform like they're on Broadway acts,
While shells chime in, joining the cracks.

A crab scuttles sideways, in slapstick ballet,
Sneaking a peek at the children who play.
Moonlight steals glances across the wet sand,
As if plotting pranks with a wave of its hand.

The horizon just giggles, painting all bright,
With colors that shimmer, a comical sight.
Mermaids are laughing, sipping their tea,
While seagulls debate if they're wild and free.

Paddling feet echo, like ducks on a porch,
As jokes fly around like they're drawn from a torch.
A deep breath of ocean, filled with pure cheer,
As the tides roll in, bringing laughter near.

Moonlit Path to Tranquility

Moonlight reflects on the waves so wide,
While beachgoers shuffle, like ducks in a stride.
Flip-flops clash in a comedic parade,
As night wraps the shore, where laughter won't fade.

A bonfire crackles with hot dog delights,
As stories unfold under starry night flights.
"Who stole my marshmallow?" comes a loud shout,
While raccoons plot heists—there's no doubt.

Shells sing their symphony, soft and sublime,
As we toast to the tales, with good friends in rhyme.
The night sky's a canvas, painted in jest,
While waves play tag with the moon in its quest.

Crickets keep time to this merry refrain,
Encircling our laughter like the soft rain.
At the end of the path, tranquility awaits,
With jokes in the air—oh, how the fun radiates!

Azure Horizons

Waves giggle with glee, they splash and they play,
Seagulls squawk jokes as they glide on their way.
Sandcastles crumble, they laugh at their fate,
As toddlers declare them a food plate for fate.

A beach ball is bouncing, a dog joins the fun,
Chasing its tail, convinced it's a run.
Sunscreen-covered humans dance in the sand,
While sunscreen slips down, oh isn't it grand?

Flip-flops are flying, what chaos ensues,
As kites swoop and dive in colorful hues.
The surfboard's a cow, or so someone said,
With pretzels for hooves, and a hot dog for bread.

Prawns serve as waiters, it's quite a delight,
Offering seaweed rolls for a midnight bite.
But watch out for jelly, it might make you slip,
As laughter erupts from a dangerous trip.

Echoes of Eternal Bliss

The sun sips a drink as it drops from the sky,
While fish flip and twirl, oh my, oh my!
Laughter carries on waves like a breeze,
Tickling the toes of the tall, silly trees.

A crab dons a hat made of seashells and flair,
As it struts its stuff, without any care.
Pineapple umbrellas, they chat on the shore,
Debating the merits of jellyfish lore.

Beach chairs reclined, like siblings that argue,
"I'm the best place, no, you just confuse!"
A picnic of goodies laid out for the crowd,
But ants stage a revolt, they are proud and loud.

With every big wave, there's a splash and a grin,
Competing for laughs, who'll lose first, who'll win?
The horizon winks, as the day starts to fade,
Reminding us all of the frolics we've made.

The Ocean's Gentle Caress

The sea whispers secrets, quite silly, quite grand,
Tickling the toes of the beach-goers' band.
Seashells telling tales of their wild ocean life,
While starfish giggle at the beach's big strife.

The tide plays peek-a-boo with the sand,
Making sandcastles vanish, oh isn't it planned?
A wave side-stepped is a glorious dance,
While flip-flops flop loudly in whimsical prance.

A rubber duck rallies the kids for a race,
While parents just lounge with sunscreen on face.
Dolphins doing backflips, they're quite the show,
With jokes about fish, that they graciously throw.

Fried doughnuts are flinging powdered supplies,
While seagulls are plotting all manner of lies.
With laughter like music, the day drifts on by,
As the sun bows down, painting laughs in the sky.

Stars Reflected on Water

As twilight unfolds, the sea starts to glow,
With winks from the stars, putting on quite a show.
A crab conducts music, with style and with flair,
While mermaids take selfies, their hair in the air.

The moon's made of cheese, or so claims the fish,
Who invite just for laughs, and a silly old wish.
Turtles doing yoga on surfboards they ride,
While rays do the limbo, and dolphins decide.

Sandy dogs chase shadows, in a wild-footed dance,
While divers are snoring, dreaming of prance.
Glowworms throw parties, they light up the night,
As crickets sing sweetly, their chirps are just right.

Reflections of laughter upon rippling seas,
Requesting our stories as soft as the breeze.
As we bask in the glow, our giggles adorn,
The world at the edge, where joy is reborn.

Spirits in the Salt Air

Seagulls gossip, they take flight,
While crabs dance under the moonlight.
A sandcastle fails at the high tide,
As the shells giggle, they cannot hide.

Beach balls bounce with a silly cheer,
A toddler trips, face full of pier.
Flip-flops flop, oh what a sound,
As laughter echoes all around.

Sandworms wiggle, putting on a show,
While sunscreen battles the sun's glow.
A dog steals fries with sneaky grace,
Leaving behind a surprised face.

When waves crash down, it's a splashy fight,
With seaweed wigs flying left and right.
But all is well in this sandy land,
Where each joy is perfectly unplanned.

Feathers of Dawn on Waves

Morning light dances, oh what a delight,
As seagulls squawk yet stay out of sight.
Coffee spills as surfers glide,
"Oops," says Joe, "There's no need to hide!"

A crab in a shell wears a tiny hat,
While kids play tag, squealing like that.
Sand in my sandwich? Quite the mistake,
A bite so crunchy, what a wake!

Kites fly high, their tails a tease,
As the breeze brings laughter with such ease.
Muffins tumble off a picnic set,
As a raccoon laughs, "Aren't I a pet?"

With waves that giggle, and suns that grin,
The day ignites with chuckles within.
Every splash tells a tale so bright,
In this joyous realm, we take flight.

Celestial Constellations Overhead

Stars twinkle, making silly faces,
As dolphins flip in odd little places.
A telescope spots a sandwich afloat,
"Aliens love mayo!" we all gloat.

The moon winks down like a cheeky mate,
While crabs argue whom to bait.
A constellation forms a fishy grin,
Whispering tales of the sea within.

Tides recite ancient, funny lore,
Of mermaids with legs who just want more.
Each shimmer on water reflects a jest,
As seagulls squabble for bread, not the rest.

With laughter echoing through night's embrace,
Each wave a giggle, each splash a grace.
In this cosmos, where whimsy thrives,
The funniest universe truly arrives.

The Essence of Peaceful Shores

Waves whisper secrets, wrapped in glee,
While beachgoers hunt for a lost flip-flop spree.
"Found it!" they shout, in triumphant cheer,
Only to see it now is a pier.

Sunbathers melt like ice cream cones,
With seagulls plotting their snacky tones.
A guy in shades slips on a crab,
The crab grins wide, "You look fab!"

Bikers zoom past with silly tunes,
Chasing down nothing beneath the moons.
A kite gets tangled in a hairdo grand,
With laughter explained, "Best flight plan!"

As sun dips low and stars appear bright,
We gather round for a funny night.
With tales of the surf and giggles galore,
Life at the beach is never a bore!

Timeless Shores and Celestial Secrets

Sandy toes and cautious crabs,
Waves crash softly on our labs.
Seagulls squawk like they own the place,
Plates of fries are hard to chase.

Buckets bright, we dig and play,
Looking for treasure, come what may.
A shell says 'hello' with a wink,
We wonder what it all could think!

Our shadows dance in sunlight's glee,
Kites and laughter fill the spree.
Rollercoasters? Nah, too much risk,
Join the line? A silly task!

Fanciful tales of swashbuckling swells,
Mermaids giggle, casting their spells.
Each grain of sand holds a chuckle,
Life's a beach; enjoy the shuffle!

Solace in Silvery Moonbeams

Beneath the stars, a dance we find,
Jumping jellyfish, oh so unkind!
Sandy beds for canine snores,
The moonlight plays, and laughter soars.

Flip-flops flung in joyous flight,
Why do we trip? Oh, what a sight!
Tide pools brim with curious glee,
A crab plays hide, then shouts, 'It's me!'

Naps are plenty, but laughter's grand,
Nearby, a toe-sucking kid took a stand!
Seagull squabbles with a stray snack,
Let's hope it gives the bird some flak.

Moonlit nights fill hearts with cheer,
Slipping on seaweed? Oh dear, oh dear!
With each wave, a giggle departs,
In silvery beams, we share our hearts.

Tide Pools of Tranquility

We peek into pools where treasures lie,
Starfish wink as you pass by.
A sea cucumber looks quite a bit confused,
Did we disturb it? It's so bemused!

Crabs in their dance display humor so bright,
Taking their vows under shimmering light.
Poking a shrimp, just to see it pout,
Who knew chic snails could really shout?

Children squeal, searching for gems,
Finding a flip-flop? Not what it seems!
Laughter meets waves; it's a perfect blend,
In salty pools, happiness knows no end.

If seaweed could talk, oh what tales it'd tell,
Of silly sunburns and odd things that fell.
With each tide that rolls, we share our delight,
A pool full of giggles, oh what a night!

A Chorus of Angels in Gentle Waves

Gentle waves hum a quirky tune,
As we build castles beneath the moon.
Dolphins giggle—what's their delight?
Splashes and laughter fill the night.

Sandcastles crumble as warnings fly,
'Run from the tide!'—a comical cry.
Kids in a splash war; water does flee,
An orchestra of giggles, wild and free.

Fluffy clouds float—they're on a quest,
To find the sun; it's quite the jest.
Inky skies steal the final light,
Close your eyes, dreams take flight.

As the tide rolls in, take one last look,
At a book full of jokes—each page a hook.
In these gentle waves, angels laugh too,
Creating fun moments; we cherish you!

In the Embrace of Ocean Breezes

The seagulls argue over fries,
Their squawks like comic surprise,
A crab waves hello in a dance,
While beach balls float in a trance.

The sunscreen dance is quite the sight,
As folks run from the waves in fright,
With flip-flops flying through the air,
Who knew that fun could lead to snare?

Kites snagged in a tangle tight,
Chasing fish, gives dogs delight,
Sandcastles wobble, what a show,
As waves crash down and take a bow.

A sandpiper struts with such grace,
Chasing tide in a curious race,
While laughter dances on the breeze,
Who needs a throne when you have these?

Coastal Symphony of the Stars

Under a blanket of sparkly skies,
Crabs play concert, what a surprise!
The moon twirls in a shimmering dress,
As jellyfish jiggle, oh, what a mess!

Starfish form a band on the shore,
Playing tunes that we all adore,
With shells as drums and waves as strings,
The ocean's laughter is what it brings.

A starry night, you might just see,
A jellybean shooting off with glee,
While sand dollars sing with such flair,
Making moments beyond compare.

In this quirky nocturnal show,
Silly sea critters put on a glow,
And as the tide whispers sweet sway,
We dance in the music 'til break of day.

Light Dancing on Water

Sunbeams waltz on the ocean's skin,
While a dolphin grins with a splashy spin,
Boogie boards skim, the surfers cheer,
As laughter trills from far and near.

Shells in a row have stories to tell,
Each one a treasure, a small wishing well,
Beachcombers search for glittering dreams,
While ice cream cones drip in sunbeam themes.

Tanning folks turn like rotisserie,
With sunscreen battles, what a mystery!
The waves giggle, they tickle our toes,
As sunlight flickers and gently glows.

When the tide slips back with a playful swish,
Mermaids plotting their next grand wish,
A splash on the beach summons all the fun,
As day turns to night, our laughs weigh a ton.

Where the Sky Meets the Sea

Clouds stretch out like a soft pillow,
While the sun drips down, a golden yellow,
Sailboats sway in a tacky tune,
While kids play tag beneath the moon.

The horizon flirts, a great illusion,
As beach umbrellas create a delusion,
With seagulls trying to steal a snack,
While we pretend we won't call back.

A splash of salt, a dab of foam,
Where barnacles build their sandy home,
Fishermen tell tales, exaggerated and bold,
While crabs exchange secrets, oh so old.

As dusk paints colors worth a cheer,
The sky winks back, bringing us near,
With laughter echoing through the air,
The silliness of life we all share.

Glistening Shores of Elysium

Waves tickle toes with a splash,
Seagulls squawk in a feathery clash,
Children build castles with great delight,
Sand in their hair, oh what a sight!

Sunbathers stretch like silly pretzels,
Mixing just right, a tan with medals,
Ice cream drips down to the sand,
Sticky fingers, life is quite grand!

A crab strolls by, looking all cool,
Onlookers laugh, he's breaking the rule,
"Oh, was that your toe?" someone shouts,
The crab just shrugs, no worries, no doubts!

As the day ends, with skies aflame,
A beach ball dances, it's quite the game,
Friends all gather for a sunset cheer,
Who needs a throne? We reign down here!

Beyond the Water's Edge

Flip-flops flying, a sight to behold,
A daring leap that's wildly bold,
The splash is epic, a tidal wave,
Watch out, folks — it's about to misbehave!

Grannies giggle in their beach hats,
While children chase after silly cats,
Dogs in shades doing a doggy paddle,
Whispers of fun, it's quite the rattle!

Someone forgot the sunscreen, oh dear,
A lobster tan brings lots of cheer,
"Next time, buddy, heed the advice,"
But oh, those crispy fries look so nice!

With laughter echoing, the sun goes low,
Surfers catch waves in a sunset glow,
A seagull swoops down for a snack,
And we all pause… for a quick bird-whack!

Blissful Breezes and Salted Air

Breezes play tricks, tousling our hair,
Sun hats blowing, just floatin' in air,
Games of frisbee turn into a mess,
Who knew a beach could be so expressive?

Shady umbrellas like mushrooms sprout,
Flipping burgers, smells drift about,
Picnics turn wild with ants any day,
"Hey, that's my sandwich!"—shoo them away!

Kites take flight, oh what a dance,
Dancing through clouds, they take their chance,
One wobbly tug, and up they soar,
Oops! Down they swoosh—what's that for?

As twilight arrives, the stars all peep,
S'mores and stories, we gather and leap,
In starlit dreams, we're beach-bound for life,
Oh, misadventures, joy without strife!

Chasing Celestial Crescendos

Surfers race waves, it's quite a sight,
Wipeouts send splashes in sheer delight,
Cheers erupt from the sandy terrain,
Who knew falling could be such a gain?

Beach volleyball—you took my serve!
As we dive and tumble, such nerve,
A netted romance blossoms in sand,
When life gives volleyball, let's all stand!

Shells sparkle bright, treasures unclaimed,
As beachcombers search, they've all gone mad,
Finding the weirdest, their treasures declare,
"Oh look, it's a flip-flop! Or maybe a bear?"

In the twilight, the bonfire glows,
Smoky marshmallows, in laughter, it flows,
Under the stars, with friends by my side,
Who needs a palace? We surf the tide!

Horizon's Edge

Seagulls squawking with delight,
A crab scuttles left and right,
The orange sun begins to grin,
While sand's a sock thief's best friend.

Buckets spill in a fishy way,
A child's laughter leads the play,
Where jellyfish waltz on the tide,
And flip-flops have nowhere to hide.

Waves crash, don't mind the splash,
Seashells hide; aren't they brash?
With a soft breeze and salty air,
Life's a beach, and we're all there.

Under umbrellas, stories weave,
With ice cream that just won't leave,
Count the stars when night arrives,
Joyful hearts, oh how we thrive!

Soulful Echoes

Bubbles rise with laughs so loud,
Fishy jokes among the crowd,
A sunburnt seagull wearing shades,
Sure knows how to dance the glades.

Sandcastles build with goofy pride,
While six-legged friends sneak inside,
A tide pool full of slimy glee,
Crustaceans laughing, can't you see?

The beach ball floats, a merry flight,
As rubber crabs join in the sight,
Dance the cha-cha if you dare,
With starfish strumming in the air.

When sunlight fades, bonfire's glow,
S'mores melting, but oh no!
Charred fingers wave in sheer delight,
Soulful echoes of the night.

The Splendor of the Cosmos in Every Ripple

Waves giggle, tickle toes in play,
Under stars, night pushes day,
A moonlit surf with jokes to share,
Surfboards flying without a care.

Planets twirling in the foam,
Each bubble sings of a far-off home,
Whales playing tag under the moon,
In a cosmic dance, they find their tune.

Twinkling lights above the shore,
With aliens asking, 'What's in store?'
A beach party through the night,
Under the stars, what a sight!

Giggles echo through the sky,
As silly dolphins leap and fly,
Each splash a giggle, each tide a cheer,
In ripples of joy, we disappear.

Celestial Currents and Gentle Breezes

A surfboard rides the cosmic wave,
Kites swoop down like they're quite brave,
As seafoam dances up the sand,
Each grain of joy, a wonderland.

Starfish wear a flashy hat,
While urging crabs to dance and chat,
Every breeze is a ticklish friend,
With giggles shared that never end.

Turtles in shades, oh what a sight,
Making shadows under starlight,
In seaweed costumes, they prance about,
Stirring laughter without a doubt.

Celestial currents pull the tide,
As laughter flows, we cannot hide,
In breezes cool, fun floats around,
With every wave, joy is found.

Rays of Hope on Sunlit Shores

Sunbeams wink like playful sprites,
As sand crabs test their new insights,
With flip-flops making quite the scene,
And ice cream cones that cause a glean.

Balloons drift high, then take a dive,
While laughter dances, all alive,
Sandwiches tossed in merry grace,
Pickles flying all over the place!

In the shallows, splashes soar,
With rubber ducks needing more,
Each tide brings giggles and delight,
Under the sun, oh what a sight!

Starry skies began to unfold,
As night brings tales, funny and bold,
With rays of joy that softly blend,
The sandy shores, our never-end.

Soft Blessings in Every Grain

In the sand, we find our snack,
Seagulls swoop, they're on the attack.
With a wink, the tide comes to tease,
Crabs in shells dance with the breeze.

Buckets filled with shells and glee,
Even fish are laughing, whee!
Sun's so bright, it wears a crown,
Making all the shadows clown.

Flip-flops squeak in joyful song,
Splashing waves say, 'Come along!'
Sandcastles rise, but often fall,
The ocean says, "You've got no wall!"

Salt in hair, and smiles abide,
Where laughter rolls like a wild tide.
Joyful moments, free from strife,
At the shore, we dance with life.

Coastal Dreams and Mystical Currents

Mermaids giggle 'neath the tide,
Finding shells, they try to hide.
Locals say they moan and sing,
As crabby kings become the bling.

Surfboards bouncing, a comical ride,
Watching wipeouts while we glide.
Oh look—a jellyfish that flies,
With all its tentacles and lies!

The beach ball, it bounces with flair,
Squeaking laughter fills the air.
Even the tide joins in the fun,
Sloshing around like it's just begun!

Funny stories in the shade,
With fruity drinks, our worries fade.
Seashells whisper secrets old,
As waves break in stories told.

The Wind's Gentle Whisper

A gust of wind, what a tickle,
Blowing hats like wild daffodils.
It plays with hair and waves goodbye,
As kites take off to touch the sky.

Laughter dances, salty air,
Sand in shorts, without a care.
Oh, how the gulls laugh and prance,
While we shimmy in a silly dance!

What's that shadow? A surfer's fall,
Paddle, paddle, laughing all.
The ocean roars a cheerful tune,
Underneath a jolly moon.

Snow cone colors bright and bold,
Sweet and cold, a taste of gold.
Every breeze a funny friend,
At this salty place, smiles never end.

Celestial Corsages of Light

Stars above, they twinkle bright,
While frogs croak a serenade at night.
We make wishes on shooting sand,
As laughter drips from sea to land.

Fireflies join in the parade,
Under the moon—the grand charade.
Crabs waltz sideways, what a sight,
Like they're practicing for a fight!

Bubbles pop with silly cheer,
In this wonderland, no fear.
Splashing joy with every splash,
As waves jump in with a joyous crash!

Stars as corsages, seashells rare,
Both giggle softly in salty air.
What a ruckus, what a plan,
At this shore, we all just jam!

Moonlit Grace on the Beach

Under the moon's watchful gaze,
The seagulls strut in a funny craze.
With crabby dance and sandy feet,
They waltz around, oh what a feat!

Waves giggle as they tickle toes,
In this scene, anything goes.
A starfish grins with a wink so sly,
"I'm the best dancer," it claims with a sigh.

Flipping shells, they make their stash,
Collecting treasures in a flash.
A jellyfish joins, what a sight,
Doing the backstroke with sheer delight!

As the night fades, laughter spreads,
The moonlight twirls on sleepy heads.
With every wave, a joyful cheer,
"Let's do this dance again next year!"

The Color of Dreams

A canvas bright, painted with glee,
Where dreams take flight, wild and free.
Lemonade skies and popcorn clouds,
Dancing sunbeams, oh my, so proud!

Sandy castles rise, but oh dear me,
A wave sneaks in, it's quite a spree!
The king's crown topples, waves laugh aloud,
"Too much swagger, you're not allowed!"

Seashells sing in colors bright,
Shouting secrets of sandy delight.
Sunburnt lobsters join the fun,
Waving claws, they're second to none!

As twilight whispers, laughter reigns,
In this wacky world where joy remains.
With every splash and every beam,
Life's a hilarious, colorful dream!

Celestial Kisses at Twilight

Stars poke fun at the sleepy sun,
Twilight giggles, it's all in good fun.
The ocean grins, with bubbles galore,
"Join my party, let's dance on the shore!"

Puddles reflect the moon's cheeky shine,
While crabs throw parties, all perfectly fine.
Seashells report the latest trends,
Wearing hats made of seaweed, no ends!

Dolphins leap with a splashy flair,
Chasing dreams in cool ocean air.
"Catch me if you can!" they playfully cry,
While starfish cheer from their rock nearby.

As night deepens, joy does too,
In this whimsical world bright and new.
With kisses of starlight and moonbeam hugs,
Laughter lingers where sand dunes snug.

Songs of the Distant Sea

A chorus rings from the vibrant shore,
Where barnacles hum and dolphins roar.
With clammy notes and a salty beat,
They serenade friends on their sandy seat.

Gulls belt out their high-pitched song,
"Isn't this happy? It won't be long!"
Shells and urchins nod in approval,
Joining this joyful, jolly removal.

As waves crash with a comic thud,
A fish shimmies through the wet, warm mud.
Tickled by seaweed, it starts to sway,
"Dance with me, my friends, come what may!"

With each refrain, the night grows bright,
Moonlit gigs bring fluffy delight.
So here's to the songs that we all share,
In this land where silliness fills the air!

A Journey to Celestial Shores

We packed our bags with snacks and glee,
Sandwiches stacked as high as a tree.
Flip-flops on, we danced with pride,
But tripped on a crab, oh what a slide!

The seagulls squawked, a chorus loud,
Claiming our fries, they were so proud.
Beach balls flew in a very wild arc,
We just hoped no one would hit the shark!

Sunburns dotted like polka dots bright,
Sunscreen was missed, oh what a sight!
Laughter erupted, waves came and went,
A beach day spent, but with much cement!

As we packed up, the sun turned to gold,
With stories to tell, we'll never grow old.
Our journey sparked giggles with every report,
Next time, we'll invest in a sturdy fort!

Sunsets on Sacred Sands

The sun dipped low, like a big round pie,
We pulled out the beach chairs, oh my, oh my!
Our drinks clinked loudly, a cheers to the sky,
Then flipped over our snacks, oh wave bye-bye!

The waves roared on, a rhythmic croon,
Just when we thought we'd get some sand-dune.
A waddle of ducks paraded in style,
Stealing our chips, oh, what a while!

Tanned legs tangled in chairs like a mess,
Debating the moon's barbecue prowess.
With laughter that echoed beyond the blue,
The sunsets painted jokes—now that's a view!

As night enveloped and stars took their place,
We dreamt we'd surf on popcorn with grace.
So here's to the vibe of shores so divine,
Where laughter and joy are forever in line!

Tranquility Beneath the Stars

Under the starlight, we spread our quilt wide,
Sipping on sodas, with the moon as our guide.
A raccoon appeared, quite a curious lad,
Swiping our snacks while we all just sat mad!

We pondered the heavens, how far they must be,
Imagining dolphins that sip iced tea.
Ghost stories echoed; we screamed with delight,
Prompting a nearby dog to join in the fright.

A sandcastle stood, a majestic delight,
Its architect stomped on it, what a sight!
Giggles replaced the solemn air,
As the tide came in, taking all with flair!

We left with a glow, under cosmic display,
With memories that tickled through laughter—hooray!
A night full of mirth, beneath countless lights,
Aces of fun, oh, those magical nights!

Starry Nights by the Shore

Stars twinkled down, as we stared in wonder,
We'd made a campfire, but lost it to thunder.
With marshmallows toasted just slightly charred,
We melted them down while others looked starred!

Footprints in sand led a puzzling race,
Whose was whose? A chaotic space!
A tide came rushing, oh what a dash,
We giggled as wet shoes called for a splash.

Seashells were gathered—such treasures, you see!
Though some turned out to be broken debris.
As we sat by the edge, in waves' gentle sway,
We mused on how crabs might dance and play.

As the lighthouse blinked with its playful beam,
We wrapped up the night like a whimsical dream.
With snorts of laughter, we left the night's glow,
How sweetly the beach offers a humorous show!

The Light Between the Currents

The gulls are squawking, what a show,
They dance like they're in a Broadway blow.
Kids build castles, then they flee,
As waves come rushing like a spree.

A crab in shades scuttles past,
Waving its claws, making a blast.
The sun's a spotlight in a vast blue,
A stage for all with a view askew.

Towels like flags in the sandy land,
Ice cream cones melting, just not as planned.
Each wave's a comedian, cracking a jest,
The shore's the punchline, we love it best.

Laughter echoes in the salty breeze,
As flip-flops fly like leaves off trees.
The scene's absurd, but we all agree,
This quirky coast is the place to be.

Sublime Reflections of the Skies

Clouds fluffy like popcorn way up high,
Tickling seagulls that zoom and fly.
A dolphin pops up, trying to mime,
A fishy ballet that's simply divine.

Sandcastles tumble, the kids all shout,
But the tide gives in with a playful pout.
A picnic of snacks, but ants join the fun,
A feast fit for all, even critters on the run.

The surfboard's a throne for a squirrel or two,
Pretending it's surfing, a marvelous view.
Beach balls collide in a colorful clash,
Laughter erupts, it's a scene full of sass.

With sunburned noses and giggles galore,
Every moment's magic, who could ask for more?
In the blissful chaos, we find our delight,
As waves roll in, oh what a sight!

Eternal Sands of Peace

Footprints tell tales of a daily spree,
Of laughter and splashes, wild and free.
Flip-flops forgotten, tossed in the tide,
A lone beach ball's straying, oh what a ride!

Dad's got a tan, but it's striped like a zebra,
He says it's chic, but we call it a diva.
Seashells are treasures, so shiny, so neat,
Yet we find more joy in the gooey sea treat.

The ice cream truck plays a tune, oh so sweet,
But it's too far away – we run on our feet!
Sandy-haired heroes with buckets in hand,
Chasing the waves in this whimsical land.

With kites in the air and toes in the sand,
The day drifts by, perfectly planned.
Smiles abound, and stories unfold,
This sandy stage is worth more than gold.

Waves of Celestial Light

Glittering water, a sparkling spree,
Playing tricks on my eyes, oh me, oh my!
A jellyfish floats, looking quite grand,
Dressed up in bubbles, it drifts with a band.

The sun wears shades as it dips in the sea,
A golden splash, so flashy and free.
Seagulls compete in a race through the air,
While beachgoers giggle, without a care.

Sunscreen battles with sand on my nose,
But laughter bursts forth as the wild wind blows.
A sand dune comedian, cracking a joke,
While light paints the scene in bright strokes of hope.

As day turns to night, we gather our chairs,
Telling old tales of our wild beach flares.
With laughter and joy, around the fire we sit,
In this delightful chaos, we just can't quit.

Ocean's Heartbeat

The waves clap hands, a noisy cheer,
Seagulls squawk, and people jeer.
A crab in a tux, looking quite grand,
Doing the cha-cha on the soft, warm sand.

A dolphin dances, flips with a grin,
While fish make faces, teasing the fin.
Sunscreen slathered, a slippery sight,
As beach balls fly with all their might!

Fried dough in hand, the seagulls dive,
Pinching snacks while we try to survive.
The ocean laughs, with a frothy spree,
Who knew a beach could host such a spree?

So grab your shades, join the fun quest,
The ocean's heartbeat steals the best dressed!
From sunburns to giggles, what a bizarre,
A trip to the beach is a laugh and a star!

Serenade of the Salted Breeze

The salty breeze plays a jazzy tune,
As sandcastles rise beneath the moon.
A clam with style, a jester at sea,
Winks curiously at you and me.

Beach towels wrinkle, sunbathers snooze,
While the waves play hide and seek in their blues.
Umbrellas dance, all colors and cheer,
As the crabs form a marching band near!

Someone's boogie board flies through the air,
Landing on a beachgoer who doesn't care.
Laughter erupts, rolling on the shore,
As the ocean serenades us more and more!

So let's ride the waves of quirky delight,
In a salt-laden dance, we take flight.
With flip-flops squeaking, we strut with ease,
Chasing the laughs in the salted breeze!

Ripples of a Dream

In watery whispers, the secrets glide,
A fish in a bowtie is on a joyride.
Gulls in tuxedos, they strut with flair,
Their beaks all agape, causing quite the scare!

The sun on the water, a glimmering show,
While dolphins perform, putting on a glow.
A sandcastle prince wears a crown made of shells,
As mermaids giggle, casting silly spells.

A beach ball battles with a gusty breeze,
As everyone tries to catch it with ease.
Children tumble and roll, with laughter galore,
In this sunny paradise, who could ask for more?

And as sunset whispers, the shadows grow long,
The ocean hums softly, a peculiar song.
With dreams intertwined in the surf's endless seam,
We float on the ripples, lost in a dream!

Secrets Beneath the Waves

Under the surface, where the fish gossip,
A clam has a secret; we must not stop!
The jellyfish floating, all translucent glee,
Swirls elegantly in a quirky spree.

Bubbles bounce high, like cheerful balloons,
As turtles play tag with the curious loons.
An octopus winks with its eight lazy arms,
Drawing sketches of beach-goers' charms.

The coral reef giggles, decorated bright,
With jokes about swimmers, oh what a sight!
Shells clink their laughter as they shift and sway,
What secrets unfold in the ocean's ballet?

So dip your toes in, let the fun start,
The waves hold the giggles in every heart.
In the world beneath, where wonders amaze,
Dive in the secrets of splashes and rays!

Tranquil Shores of Dawn

Seagulls squawk with morning cheer,
While flip-flops dance, oh so near.
The ocean waves have trouble sleeping,
While sandcastles are busy weeping.

A crab in shades, with style so bold,
Claims his throne on grains of gold.
Shells gossip tales of days gone by,
As sunbeams wink, the fish nearby.

Beach towels spread like magic carpets,
Where sunscreen's the brush for sun-kissed artists.
Laughter bubbles like fizz in a drink,
As children plot with mischief to think.

So grab your float and take a ride,
On a sea of giggles, where fun won't hide.
The dawn's calm hug, a playful tease,
In this blissful chaos, we find our ease.

Where Waves Kiss the Sky

Up high, the kites chase clouds with flair,
While swimmers splash without a care.
The dolphins leap, with laughter loud,
Mocking the sun, oh, what a crowd!

Sandy toes and salty hair,
Let's build a kingdom, don't you dare!
Invasive seagulls plan a steal,
As snacks take flight, what a shocking deal!

The tide rolls in, a slippery blunder,
What lives below? Oh, wait for thunder!
Jellyfish waltz in a flowing gown,
While crabs perfect their moonwalk down.

Giggles echo as waves puff and sigh,
Sunscreen looks like a slip 'n' slide!
Tonight's bonfire lights up the night,
With marshmallows dancing, pure delight!

Celestial Reflections

Mirrors gleam where water meets sand,
Stars argue over who's the best brand.
As night unfolds, fish tell their tales,
Of moonlit journeys, oceanic gales.

A paddleboard floats, a laughing beast,
While raccoons plot a midnight feast.
Turtles in capes attend the show,
As the swirling tide begins to flow.

Sipping coconuts that bounce like balls,
While whales try out for phantom calls.
The lighthouse blinks like a cheeky eye,
Winking at ships that drift on by.

Under bright stars, oh what a sight,
Sailboats giggle in the pale moonlight.
With nature's band playing soft tonight,
The shore's a stage, oh what a delight!

A Shoreline Reverie

Footprints chase each other in sand,
As crabs play tag, so unplanned.
Waves crash down with a comic flip,
While beach hats are lost in a wild trip.

Kites tangle high, what a colorful mess,
As seagulls demand their sugary press.
The breeze carries laughter on its back,
With jellybeans rolling off the snack rack.

Strange seashells whisper silly charms,
While surfers ride with acrobatic arms.
Each splash a note in a song of glee,
As laughter swirls like a dance with the sea.

So come embrace this sandy jest,
Where each jest is a daydream quest.
In this joyful realm, let's take a seat,
And let the shore hum its funny beat.

Whispers from the Tide's Embrace

The waves come in with giggles loud,
Shells play tag beneath the crowd.
Seagulls squawk with endless glee,
As crabs dance like they're on spree.

The sun wears shades, what a sight,
A beach ball rolls with pure delight.
Flip-flops fly in a sandy race,
While kids build castles, grins on their face.

A starfish winks, a mermaid grins,
Tide pools bubble—let the fun begin!
Swimmers splash like porpoises near,
As laughter echoes, loud and clear.

The shore's a circus, full of cheer,
With every wave, there's nothing to fear.
We dive and twirl, beneath the sun,
In this joyful place, we all are one.

The Sacred Confluence of Sky and Sea

Clouds float by like marshmallow fluff,
Waves whisper secrets, never too rough.
A dolphin leaps, with a wink and a spin,
So much action, let the beach games begin!

Kites soar high, like not-so-quiet planes,
While sandcastles hold imaginary reigns.
Picnics spread as ants plot their heist,
Finding crumbs for their grand beach feast, oh so nice!

The sun turns pink, a comedy show,
While beachgoers dance, putting on a glow.
"Watch me flip!" someone calls with flair,
Splashdown! Water goes everywhere!

A treasure map scrawled on a napkin bright,
Leads to ice cream cones, oh what a sight!
Seashells exchanged for jokes and laughter,
In this place full of joy, we find our after.

Cosmic Reflections on Serene Waters

Stars peek down, like eternal scouts,
While fish gossip in playful shouts.
A boat rocks gently, a swaying tale,
With seaweed beards that'd never fail.

Moonlight dances on waves of giggles,
As the tide tickles and wiggles.
A hermit crab dons a conch for a hat,
While jellyfish drift, avoiding the chat.

In the distance, a foghorn toots,
Echoing laughter in goofy hoots.
A beach cat surveys her kingdom bold,
Claiming fishy treasures worth more than gold.

Nighttime brings a whole new scheme,
With starfish waltzing in a dreamy dream.
Between waves and moonlight's shimmering bliss,
Each moment is funny; it's hard to miss!

Tranquility Found between Earth and Sky

A sand dune whispers, "Come take a seat,"
Where flip-flops pile up like scattered feet.
Umbrellas of colors blush and flare,
As picnics unfold without a care.

Waves crash down with a bubbly cheer,
As umbrellas dance, drawing near.
A furry dog digs for buried treasure,
While kids squeal in complete measure.

Sunset sparkles in shades of silliness,
As beachgoers lounge in sheer blissfulness.
Chased by tides, a frisbee flies,
Landing near a crab who feigns surprise!

Finally, as stars twinkle and stretch,
Sandy feet wiggle like they've met.
For in this place of joyful bliss,
Life is a party that we can't miss!

www.ingramcontent.com/pod-product-compliance
Lightning Source LLC
Chambersburg PA
CBHW072124070526
44585CB00016B/1552